For Ken

From: John

A New Relationship to Money in 100 Days

A New Relationship to Money in 100 Days

Yohan Mohammed

Published by Tablo

For my mother,

who always reminds me of what's possible,

and for my father,

who says nothing when I dream up the impossible.

Introduction

Let's get one thing straight at the beginning, this journal doesn't have any special secrets. There aren't any formulas or special practices to create a new relationship. What there is, is work, that will change your relationship to money and your life in the process. As you work through the different pieces of this journal you'll notice a lot of freedom to create whatever you wish. This is the design and intention of the journal: to give you absolute freedom in how you would like to design your life. For many people this might come naturally and for others this might be more challenging. The basic design is simply to read through the writing prompts each day and write your ideas and answers.

Each day will also include an activity related to the writing prompt and will allow you to flex the muscle discussed that day. Between the questions and activities are lines as well as blank space to write or create anything. Whether it takes you 100 days or 100 weeks, the success of this journal will be based on how much you put into it. Each day you will have to make choices about yourself, the people in your life and your finances. Make choices that drive you to be bigger than you are, create things even you may not think possible, and include the people you had no idea would support you.

There is an easy, medium and hard way to complete this journal. The level you choose will result in the rewards you gain at the end. For those looking for the easy route you will complete the journal as designed, you will gain insights, and design a future very similar to the one you currently have. Nothing is wrong with this and yet there is something to taking the road less traveled, the road you might fear, the road even you didn't see yourself on. For those of you that choose medium, there will be areas you absolutely excel in, thrive on and enjoy. There will also be areas that are boring, make no difference and have you simply writing to get to the next page. Based on participating this way it can be asserted that this is exactly how your life is going right now. There are areas of sunshine and areas of gloom. Interrupt this and design a future worth living for. For those of you that choose hard you may pick up the journal and stop at the first day. This journal may take you a couple times to get started again, maybe even sit on the to-do list for a long time before you really dig in.

Don't look at this journal and its freedoms and choices as easy, medium or hard. Instead when you have the freedom to create for yourself, think about the one thing that would stretch you to the fullest, what you fear doing, what's been on your mind, but you just haven't taken the leap of faith on. Do that!

When you have the freedom to include others, whether it be sharing, creating a community, or simply observing, the place to stand in is where do I feel the most uncomfortable, not a setting you are already familiar with. People will surprise you, in what they share when you are really listening. People will surprise you, in the resources and guidance they have and are willing to offer when they know you are being genuine. People will surprise you in supporting your ideas and goals, when they are truly included and trust the road you've chosen.

Finally when it comes to your finances, money can help or hinder. It can control you or you can control it. When you have the freedom to make choices around your finances, always invest in yourself first as it will always pay the most dividends. See money as a tool you can use to create rather than as a medium to purchase items.

Money is directly linked to the trust you have in yourself, the trust you have in others and the trust that others have in you. Grow yourself, the trust you have in yourself and others and your finances will follow. Let's begin . . .

Day 1

Everything begins and ends with a vision, so this is where we will begin as well. Like everything else in this journal, we will focus on one thing at a time. Creating a 5 year vision over the next couple days, today we begin with the person you want to become. What will people say about you in 5 years? Who will you be known as? Try writing this in the past tense, so from the perspective that this is who you already are, write below who you are in the world 5 years from now. Use the prompts to discover someone new in yourself.

- I am . . .
- I created . . .
- I have achieved . . .

_____

_____

_____

_____

_____

_____

_____

_____

_____

_____

_____

Activity

Keep what you've written in mind throughout your day. Thinking from the perspective that you are already this new person, ask:

Would that person be doing what I'm doing today? Reflect on this below.

_____

_____

_____

_____

_____

_____

_____

_____

_____

_____

Day 2

What would you be doing for a living if you could do anything in your life? Now think for a second that you're already doing it. How does it feel to be getting up each day doing exactly what you'd love to be doing? Write about what you love doing most. Finish the following sentences:

- At some point I knew I'd love doing . . .

- When I began doing . . .

- I can't remember a day where I wasn't doing . . .

_____

_____

_____

_____

_____

_____

_____

_____

_____

_____

Activity

What you wrote about and what you're currently doing, how different are they? Can you see yourself doing this everyday? Are there opportunities to test whether you'd enjoy this everyday? Throughout your day, reflect on how life will be different 5 years from now. Write down what you thought below.

_____

_____

_____

_____

_____

_____

_____

_____

_____

_____

_____

_____

_____

_____

Day 3

Where will you be in 5 years, not mentally, but physically. Where will you actually be? What does it look like? Smell like? Again, write in the past tense as though this place is familiar, you've already been here, you've always been here. Use the prompts to help.

- I remember the first time I saw . . .

- It sounded like . . .

- It smelt like . . .

- I felt . . .

_____

_____

_____

_____

_____

_____

_____

_____

_____

_____

Activity

Notice the settings you're in today. How long do you spend time there? How long do you plan to continue being there? Notice anything about these settings that you enjoy or do not enjoy. Reflect on your observations below.

_____

_____

_____

_____

_____

_____

_____

_____

_____

_____

_____

_____

_____

Day 4

Who will be in your life 5 years from now? It could be people who already exist in your life or people you wish to meet and include. Use the prompts to create the people around you in the future.

- The most important people around me have been . . .

- Together we created . . .

- As a community we achieved . . .

_____

_____

_____

_____

_____

_____

_____

_____

_____

_____

Activity

Are all the people you wrote about above already in your life? If so, observe your interactions with them today. If there are new people you've included, think about where you will find them. Do the places you frequent currently include these people, or will you need to discover new places? Reflect on your findings below.

_____

_____

_____

_____

_____

_____

_____

_____

_____

_____

_____

_____

_____

Day 5

What are the people in your life doing in their own lives? Are you aware that it's no coincidence, that you are, where you are in your life, because of the people around you? The same is true for those people. They are, where they are in their life because of who you are to them. Based on what you're doing for a living 5 years from now, how has that changed the lives of those around you? Maybe you've created a company with them and now everyone around you works together. Or maybe your work impacts many different communities, not just your own. Write about what you are doing, what you absolutely enjoy doing and how that has already changed the lives of those around you. Use the prompts to support:

- The people around me initially thought . . .

- Together we chose to . . .

- Together we created . . .

- Together we accomplished . . .

_____

_____

_____

_____

_____

_____

_____

_____

_____

_____

_____

Activity

Observe the people in your life today. How happy or unhappy are they? Could you make their life a little better today, out of your actions? Small actions can bring happiness for a short time. Larger, long term actions can bring happiness for a lifetime. Reflect on what you will to bring to those people in your life.

_____

_____

_____

_____

_____

_____

_____

_____

_____

Day 6

Where are the people in your life, physically? Does your immediate family live close by or are you oceans apart? Write as though everyone is exactly where they need to be. Do you prefer to live on an island alone? Or maybe a major city? Do you have a single home? Or many? Thinking that the people in your life are exactly where they need to be, write as though they are already there.

- My family members live . . .

- My friends live . . .

- We all . . .

_____

_____

_____

_____

_____

_____

_____

_____

_____

_____

_____

Activity

Listen today to the people around you as they discuss where they live, their commute, where they go. Create conversations around where people would like to live, how far they'd like to be from work and where they might vacation. Observe those people actively working towards doing something about it, compared to the people that just complain about it. Reflect on your conversations and observations.

_____

_____

_____

_____

_____

_____

_____

_____

_____

_____

_____

Day 7

You've spent some time looking at who you will be in your vision, what you will be doing and where you will be. Now we will create how you're going to get there. When creating the how, write from the perspective that you already have what you need. Too often we look elsewhere because we don't believe we have what we need. We don't have the knowledge, the resources, the money, etc. Today, write as though those things were already available, and this is how your vision came to be.

- I thought I needed . . .

- It was very important having . . .

- What made all the difference was . . .

_____

_____

_____

_____

_____

_____

_____

_____

_____

_____

_____

Activity

Listen to the people around you today, when they want to do something new, create something, try something. Listen for what stops them immediately. Key words or wording could include, "but," "I don't know," "it's always been that way," "that never changes." etc. Reflect on what you've heard.

_____

_____

_____

_____

_____

_____

_____

_____

_____

_____

Day 8

It's been a week of creating a vision. We've discussed things like: who you will be, what you see for yourself in the future and where you see the people around you. We've also begun writing in the past tense, like it's already happened. I'd like to acknowledge you for getting this far. Some people may have started strong and stopped a couple of days in, others may have gotten through each day, but didn't have time to really complete the activities. What today is about is a fundamental lesson in life. One that has guided everyone at one point or another. It's also something that will happen every now and again as it is very important. Today we look at failure.

Failure is something we all go through at many times in our lives, but as we get older, the fear of failing grows more and more. Until we somehow create for ourselves that failure is no longer an option, so we would rather not even begin.

So let's be clear, **you will fail often throughout this journal**.

Failing is a good thing.

Actually, its a great thing and will be necessary before you can design the life you want. If you assume that doing exactly what you're doing now will somehow get you to a different life, let's burst that bubble now. Doing exactly what you're doing now, will get you exactly what you have right now. Doing something different will get you something different. This is fundamentally simple, yet extraordinarily hard to do.

Therefore today is not about creating anything, we will leave that to tomorrow. Today, review your previous entries, add to them if you need to. Start over maybe, take a day or two to redo something you felt you might have missed. Or, refine what you've been writing about all week, polish the important points and expand on areas you wish you had time to before. Take a break to look at what you've accomplished so far and take a moment to acknowledge that you've done some good work. Remember that the start of every journey begins with a few steps and you've just taken the first few towards an incredible new future of your own design.

Day 9

Taking everything from the beginning of this journal so far, we will create a personal vision to encompass all aspects of what your life will look like in 5 years. Like everything else, we will be writing this from a position in the future, as though this has already happened. Take the time you need to really dig into everything you created so far. Most of your writing has been functional, using the writing prompts, and sectional, writing from each day. Today, bring it all together and create a future that you can see, touch, taste and feel. Write it from the position that it has already happened, using the past tense. Write so vividly that if spoken to someone, they would be able to experience it with you.

My Vision

_____

_____

_____

_____

_____

_____

_____

_____

_____

_____

_____

_____

_____

_____

_____

Vision Activity

Share your vision with someone today. If they have questions, or don't completely understand something, edit what you've written. Do this with 3 separate people, continuing to edit when anything is unclear. It is important to remember that even if everything makes sense to you, without the support of others nothing can be achieved. Therefore, we need to ensure that your vision can be understood by the people around you.

Routines

Routines are something we all perform. Whether we know it or not we've taken routines from our parents, close friends, even coworkers. Routines drive our daily lives where they can set us up for success or failure. Being able to integrate new routines is paramount to character development and throughout this journal you will be creating new routines for yourself.

Let's face it, the routines you've been performing have gotten you here. You want to elevate yourself to the next version of you. That means your routines need to elevate as well or in some cases you simply need new routines.

The word routine is derived from the French word "route" meaning road which is very fitting as we look at the road ahead. You will be creating new routines for yourself, the people around you and your finances.

Let's Begin...

Day 10

Today, we begin creating new routines that will snowball into a complete new direction for your future. Starting with yourself, what is one new daily routine you've always wanted to start? It could be absolutely anything, but it must be something you do for yourself. Maybe it's going to the gym, or reading a new book, one page or one chapter each day. Maybe it's just going for a walk, or waking up at a specific time everyday. Write below what the new routine is that you will take on and why. Most often we take the time to build and grow relationships with others, but we don't take the time to take care of ourselves. This personal routine with be a new relationship you will have with yourself.

_____

_____

_____

_____

_____

_____

_____

_____

_____

_____

_____

Activity

Is there anything in your life that will be impacted by this new routine? Do you need to get to bed earlier to be up at a specific time? Do you need to buy the book you intend to read. Whatever you need, to begin this routine, reflect on whether this routine makes sense before you begin tomorrow. Revise if necessary.

_____

_____

_____

_____

_____

_____

_____

_____

_____

_____

_____

Day 11

Today is the first day you will put your new personal routine into action. With anything new, there will always be fear and concern. With anything you've created so far, it must be worth doing regardless of the fear and concerns you might have. Write down all the fears and concerns you have about this new personal routine. What you know about yourself when it comes to trying something new? How do you see yourself in the space of newness, the unknown, or simply sticking with something?

_____

_____

_____

_____

_____

_____

_____

_____

_____

_____

_____

Activity

Perform your personal routine today. Was it as easy or as challenging as you expected? Do you see yourself sticking with it? What, if anything, could stop you from completing it every day. It is important to make this work for you, so revise or edit as needed while still sticking to what you said you would do.

_____

_____

_____

_____

_____

_____

_____

_____

_____

_____

_____

_____

_____

_____

Day 12

In the same fashion we created our vision for the future, we started looking at our own life, then the lives of people around us. We will do the same when creating a new routine, but instead of the routine simply involving ourselves, we will begin to include other people. The creation of this new community routine must involve someone else. Similar to the new relationship you created with yourself by committing to a new personal routine, the community routine will allow you to commit yourself to someone else. It could include creating a new community, joining a club, or simply spending time with your friends and/or family. As this routine will involve someone else, complete it daily or weekly, but not something monthly or quarterly. Remember, building anything should be done regularly, therefore building a new relationship should not be treated any differently. Use the space below to brainstorm this new community routine.

_____

_____

_____

_____

_____

_____

_____

_____

_____

_____

_____

Activity

What will it take to fulfill this routine? Who do you want to include, is it one person or many? Regardless of your choice, what will it take to make this commitment and stick with it? Unlike the personal routine if you forget or simply stop, it only affects you. Quitting the community routine will not only affect your trust in yourself, but also the trust others have for you. Ensure you choose something worthwhile.

_____

_____

_____

_____

_____

_____

_____

_____

_____

Day 13

Depending on whether your new community routine is something you can start right away or something you start next week, it is still important to declare it. That declaration, much like your personal routine, comes with new fears and concerns. What is different is these fears and concerns involve others and bring with them an elevated concern. "What will people think, say, etc. about me?" Below, declare your new community routine. What does it look like, what is involved and why have you chosen it?

_____

_____

_____

_____

_____

_____

_____

_____

_____

_____

_____

Activity

What fears and concerns do you have about fulfilling this community routine? What is the worst thing someone could think of you? What is the worst thing someone could say to you? Reflect on what you would think if someone thought or said these things to you or to someone else about you.

_____

_____

_____

_____

_____

_____

_____

_____

_____

_____

_____

_____

_____

Day 14

We've finally come to the first day we begin to think about finances. Some may have assumed that this journal would start with ways to build or grow a financial future. That assumption would be completely incorrect. To build anything requires the foundation of a vision and a community first. This is why we spent our time there. Why do you think creating a vision first might support a stronger foundation for your finances? Why do you think creating a community first might support a stronger foundation for your finances?

_____

_____

_____

_____

_____

_____

_____

_____

_____

Activity

Notice how you view your life through the lens of your finances. Does the amount of money you have define who you are? Does your community define who you are? Do you define who you are?

_____

_____

_____

_____

_____

_____

_____

_____

_____

_____

_____

_____

_____

_____

Day 15

Today, we begin to think through a new financial routine. In the same vein as the personal and community routines, the financial routine allows you to begin a new relationship with money. This financial routine should be done daily or weekly, therefore think through what new routine you will explore. This routine must be something you do to grow or expand your finances. Simply checking your accounts regularly or moving funds to a single account does not count. Instead these are things that can be done to better structure your finances. This routine needs to be something you can do repeatedly. It could be saving a dollar each day, or putting aside money each week, bringing a lunch rather than buying one and saving the money, or removing one regularly occurring activity that has a cost like dinner out or the movies. Regardless of the action, it must impact your finances regularly in order to be measured and for you to be able to see changes.

_____

_____

_____

_____

Activity

When you hear the word money, what's the first thing that comes to mind? Write that down. What do you believe about money? What are your opinions about money? Ask others the same questions today. Reflect on your answers and theirs below.

_____

_____

_____

_____

_____

_____

_____

_____

_____

_____

Day 16

Now that you've chosen your financial routine, it may be some time before you can begin. Whether it be tomorrow or next week, what are your genuine fears and concerns about yourself and your finances? Is money something that comes to you easily? Is it available or unavailable? What do you think of yourself and your financial situation? What do you think about others and their financial situation? How do you compare yourself to others based on money and finances?

Activity

What are your fears and concerns about money? What would be the worst thing to happen to you financially? What would be worse, that thing actually happening or people thinking it happened to you? Reflect on these questions below.

_____

_____

_____

_____

_____

_____

_____

_____

_____

_____

_____

_____

_____

_____

Budget

Budgets are an integral piece to financial success. Over the next little while we will focus on three main themes as it relates to budgeting. We will spend time focusing and understanding all the different expenses in our lives. Accepting that expenses exist and have a role to play in our financial success is very important. From small expenses to large expenses and even unknown expenses, it's always best to be prepared and have a plan. Next we'll focus on cash flow. For many of us one source of income is the norm and is usually never enough to sustain us. We will look at different sources of income and how it can best be used to grow your finances. Finally we'll look at savings and how you can save, even small amounts, that will secure your future. We will engage each theme through the different routines we've chosen to perform continuing to look at building ourselves, our relationships and our finances. Let's Begin...

Day 17- Expenses

As we begin to look at creating a budget, we will start with expenses. Today we will look at small expenses. These are the expenses that you may not even see as expenses, items like your morning coffee or your weekly lottery ticket. They are usually less than $5 or $10 in cost and/or may happen frequently like daily or weekly. In most cases, we don't see these as expenses as they're just part of our regular day. But, if you spend $5 a day on coffee, that's nearly $2000 a year. What cost do you consider a small expense? Think back in your life to the time you were first given money. How much was it? Who gave it to you? What did it mean to you to receive it? What did that person mean to you? What did you spend it on? Whatever amount it was, would it be considered a lot or a little money to you today? How have you changed since then and what you consider a lot or a little money?

_____

_____

_____

_____

_____

_____

_____

_____

_____

_____

_____

Activity

As you go through your day, simply notice all the minor expenses you pay for. Write these expenses below and reflect on when this became a regular expense. Why did it become a regular expense? Does it need to continue to be an expense?

_____

_____

_____

_____

_____

_____

_____

_____

_____

_____

Day 18

We are all familiar with large expenses. They might be for health or medical reasons or something you've been saving for. Large expenses, will differ in amount and frequency based on the person, but the inevitable truth is that we all have them. I'm sure right now there is something you're saving for, something you're paying off, or something you don't even know how you will purchase, but you definitely need it. As we grow up, these expenses may start from books for school all the way to your first car or home. What doesn't change is the fact that the amount grows. Can you remember the first time an expense felt large? The first time you had to save up for something? Or the first time you had to create a plan to make that purchase? How were you able to make the purchase? What did it take? Explain below.

_____

_____

_____

_____

_____

_____

_____

_____

_____

_____

_____

Activity

Take some time today to write down all the large expenses you've had this year. Write down all the large expenses you know are coming up. Be sure to include the complete costs, with taxes, fees, etc.

_____

_____

_____

_____

_____

_____

_____

_____

_____

_____

_____

Day 19

Medium expenses are not something that people think about. Usually we speak in terms of small and large expenses and usually spend much more time discussing the large ones. There are expenses that exist in between though. These are the expenses that may not happen frequently and they may not be something you complain about, but instead you justify them. This could include car expenses, dinners out, even the movies to some extent could be considered a medium expense. Medium expenses usually involve another person, like in the case of dinners out or going to the movies and usually cost more than $10-$20. Think back to the first time you felt you had to pay for another person. What was the expense? Did you have a good time? Why did you think it was your responsibility to pay? Was paying for the other person discussed with that person or was it a surprise? Reflect on why you pay for others.

_____

_____

_____

_____

_____

_____

_____

_____

_____

_____

_____

_____

Activity

As you go through your day, pay for someone else. Choose whether your gift will be known or anonymous. It could be a coffee, lunch or something else. Take note of how it felt to pay for another, what was their reaction? What did you expect compared to what happened? How did it make you feel? Describe below.

_____

_____

_____

_____

_____

_____

_____

_____

_____

_____

Day 20

Long term expenses can be any size: small, medium or large. What they are, is forever. These expenses last longer than a marriage in most cases and stick with you through various stages of life. These can include car payments or mortgages, but more and more simple services are creeping up into the state of a long term expense. Music services, software subscriptions, and video services to name a few are becoming expenses that will in most cases last a lifetime. When did it, or has it, ever occurred to you that you might be paying for something forever? If this has happened in the past, reflect on what reasons or explanations you used to make it okay. If it has just dawned on you that you'd be paying for Netflix forever, how does it feel? Do you ever see yourself ending your long term expenses? What would it feel like to never have long term expenses?

_____

_____

_____

_____

_____

_____

_____

Activity

Today, think through and list all of your long term expenses. A long term expense can include something you have control over ending, but would you ever actually end it? Long term expenses should can be defined as having payments longer than 2-5 years.

Day 21

Short term expenses are actually harder to define than long term expenses. They don't last forever but include items like short term loans or purchases that might be paid on credit. For example, a house can be a long term expense, but the appliances bought for it are short term expenses paid over a period less than 5 years. Cell phones are also contracted in such a way that the payment ends at a certain point, but inevitably we change plans or change phones, so this could become a long term expense. Think through your short term expenses, why did you take them on? In some cases, they are needed right away as in the case of appliances, but think through whether these expenses were needed right away or if they could have waited and become more of a single large purchase. Find an example of a short term expense where you ended paying it off. How did it feel to complete that payment? What did you do with the extra money afterward?

_____

_____

_____

_____

_____

_____

_____

_____

_____

_____

_____

Activity

List out the short term expenses you've had in the past. Reflect on the amount of time it took to pay them off. If you were still paying for them now, how much would you be paying? Since you are not paying that now, what could you be using the money for?

_____

_____

_____

_____

_____

_____

_____

_____

_____

Day 22

Unknown expenses. You know what I'm talking about. The one that just popped up and you forget about. The one that you'd been putting off and now it needs to be paid. The one where you've been saving really well and it's exactly the amount needed to pay for this surprise unknown expense. Regardless of how unknown these expenses are, accidents happen. Life happens. These are the expenses that just don't give you a break. When was the first time you'd been saving for something specific only to have it used for a completely different purpose because of an accident or something came up? Did you ever end up getting the item you were saving up for? What did you start to believe about saving when that happened?

_____

_____

_____

_____

_____

_____

_____

_____

_____

_____

_____

Activity

Think about the most recent unknown expense that came up.
Reflect on how it was brought to your attention and how you felt
about it. What did you do about it? What have you done around
saving since that unknown expense?

_____

_____

_____

_____

_____

_____

_____

_____

_____

_____

_____

Day 23

Today we're going to look back at that personal routine you created a while back. How has it been going? Have you kept up with it? New routines added to our everyday lives can be some of the most difficult things we do. The routines we have today started somewhere, but we rarely think about them now. In most cases they were imposed on us, or they just made sense, like getting up at a decent time for work. It's perfectly fine if you have taken no action on your personal routine. What isn't perfectly fine is if you make it mean that you can not complete it, or in some way you believe you're incapable of sticking with it. Reflect on your thoughts about yourself and discover how you really feel, what's underneath your immediate reaction? If you've kept your promise to yourself and your personal routine has been performed consistently since you created it, reflect on your experiences so far. What thoughts do you have about yourself in being able to continue this routine each day? What changes has it made, how do you feel, and will you continue it?

_____

_____

_____

_____

_____

_____

_____

_____

_____

_____

_____

Activity

Take a moment to think about the personal routine you chose. Does it have a cost? Is there an expense involved even if indirectly. Reflect on how this personal routine has affected your expenses.

_____

_____

_____

_____

_____

_____

_____

_____

_____

_____

Day 24

Looking back to the fears and concerns you had about taking on a personal routine, did any of those fears show up? Was the fear not sticking with your personal routine? If a fear or concern broke through while you were performing your personal routine, reflect on it below. Does the fact that it happened prove that you're right? Where else in your life do you have to be right? In this case, being right has cost you not being able to perform your personal routine. Where else has being right cost you something? If your fears and concerns did not show up, what would your life and your personal routine look like? Fears and concerns should never limit you from taking moving forward. By sticking to a routine and not having your fears and concerns follow, you are on the path to a different result. Discuss how you feel about this new path, and what new fears and concerns may be showing up for you.

_____

_____

_____

_____

_____

_____

_____

_____

_____

_____

_____

_____

Activity

List out the times you've been right and what you got out of it. List the times you've been wrong and what you got out of it. Reflect on that list.

_____

_____

_____

_____

_____

_____

_____

_____

_____

_____

Day 25

The community routine you created was required to involve at least one other person. Did you stick with it? Have you been keeping up with the routine? If you haven't stuck with it, you've now included others in your inability to stick to something. Reflect on how that feels and what you can do to regain the trust that your routine is intended to build. If you stuck with it, how did you do it, what did it take to keep your word and what have you learned so far. Reflect on the trust between you and the community you've chosen (whether that be one person or a group of people).

_____

_____

_____

_____

_____

_____

_____

_____

_____

_____

Activity

Has your community routine become an expense? If it is an expense, what kind is it? Small, large, long term, etc. Remember, even making a new friend and meeting for coffee has an expense, albeit a small one. If it isn't a monetary expense, you are now giving time to another person. Discover what value you place on your time, and describe your experiences with your community routine so far.

_____

_____

_____

_____

_____

_____

_____

_____

_____

_____

_____

_____

Day 26

Did your fears and concerns show up during your community routine or not? Whether they showed up or not, what have you learned? What does it mean to you? How does it affect your routine? Do you feel like continuing? Or do you feel like creating a new community routine? Both options are perfectly alright. Regardless of whether you stick it out or try something new, what may be new fears and concerns? Sticking with it could mean the fear of it getting worse or never happening the way you intended. Creating a new routine could just bring back the same fears you had before. Discuss below.

_____

_____

_____

_____

_____

_____

_____

_____

_____

_____

Activity

If you choose to stick with your routine, create structures to stick with it or enhance your participation. If you choose a new routine, create structures to participate and maintain regular participation.

_____

_____

_____

_____

_____

_____

_____

_____

_____

_____

_____

_____

_____

_____

Day 27

Your personal routine was meant to expand your relationship with yourself and your community routine was meant to expand your relationship with others. The financial routine was meant to expand your relationship with money. Have you kept up with your financial routine? How have your finances changed since beginning? Whether you stuck with it or not, explain what you've learned so far. What do you believe about yourself having stuck with your financial routine or not? Is this different from what you believe about yourself from the other two routines?

_____

_____

_____

_____

_____

_____

_____

_____

_____

_____

Activity

Reflecting on your financial routine, how does it affect your expenses. Have you structured your bills differently, does that give you more money in your account for a specific period of time? Whatever you chose as your financial routine, discover how its affected your expenses and explain what it will mean for your future.

_____

_____

_____

_____

_____

_____

_____

_____

_____

_____

_____

_____

_____

Day 28

Which expense is the most concerning to you? Was it the small expenses, the silent killers, or the unknown expenses? Regardless of what was most concerning, expenses exist and will continue to exist in your life. What you can do to overcome them, is simply accept the fact that they exist and form a plan. The fears and concerns you described about taking on a financial routine, did they include or involve expenses? Describe ways you see yourself being comfortable with expenses of any kind (small, large, long term, short term) and what it will take to make that a reality.

_____

_____

_____

_____

_____

_____

_____

_____

_____

_____

Activity

Discover different things you can do to ensure expenses of any
type are no longer a fear or concern. What would it feel like if
expenses were something positive, something necessary,
something you needed to live. Reflect on how you would feel if that
were included in your vision.

_____

_____

_____

_____

_____

_____

_____

_____

_____

_____

_____

_____

_____

Day 29- Income

What is your main source of income? What did it take to get you to this moment right now? From education to internships to your first job to today, reflect on your main source of income. Take a moment to acknowledge yourself for what it took to get here. Regardless of whether you see your current situation as something good or bad, the work you've put in has gotten you to this place. It will take more work to get to the next step, but for now let's be honest about how far we've come.

_____

_____

_____

_____

_____

_____

_____

_____

_____

_____

Activity

As you continue your day, observe where your main source of income comes from. How reliable is it and how much do you rely on it? Is this your only source? What would happen without it? How do you use your main source of income? Explain

_____

_____

_____

_____

_____

_____

_____

_____

_____

_____

_____

_____

_____

_____

_____

Day 30

For some, their main source of income is not enough. Therefore, they have a second income. It might be a part time job, it might be freelance work, just something that supplements their current income. If you currently have a secondary income, explain what it is, when you first took it on and why you felt you needed it. If you do not have a second income, would you like one? Where could it come from? Is it something you would be able to take on?

_____

_____

_____

_____

_____

_____

_____

_____

_____

_____

Activity

Everyone likes the idea of a little extra money, what would you do with a second income? Spend the day looking at what could be possible with some extra money. Discuss below.

_____

_____

_____

_____

_____

_____

_____

_____

_____

_____

_____

_____

_____

_____

Day 31

We've looked at primary income and secondary income, but what if there was more? What if you had multiple sources of income? Statistics suggest that most millionaires have at least 7 sources of income. There are two different types of income: active and passive. Active income includes wages, commissions, salaries, etc. Passive income includes investments, royalties, rental income, etc. Do some research if you have to and list all the different ways you believe you could gain different streams of income. Discuss your findings and reflect on which ones may be more appealing to you and why.

_____

_____

_____

_____

_____

_____

_____

_____

_____

_____

Activity

Looking at all the different sources of income you came up with, which one seems the easiest to dig into? Which source do you truly believe you can take on, create, work through and be successful in? Start there. The structures we've already created and will continue to discuss can be duplicated as a game plan for this new source of income. It can be duplicated over and over again for however many different sources of income you wish to take on. Would you be willing to put in the work to duplicate the process over and over again?

_____

_____

_____

_____

_____

_____

_____

_____

_____

_____

_____

Day 32

Surprise income. Everyone likes a surprise, something they weren't expecting. Just as fast as a surprise can happen, it can also disappear. Review the first time you received surprise money (possibly as a child), how did you feel, what did you make it mean and what did you do with it? Compare that with the last time you received surprise income (possibly a work bonus or tax return), was your reaction the same, different or did you do something differently? Explore that below.

_____

_____

_____

_____

_____

_____

_____

_____

_____

_____

_____

Activity

What if you were to receive surprise income today? Where would it come from? What would the amount be? Now, reflect on what you created, the amount you chose. How far fetched is the surprise income and what was the amount? Do you often create far fetched ideas? Do you do this knowing it can not be achieved or maybe goals like this drive you to push through your mental ceiling? In contrast do you lower your own expectations of yourself and what your capable of? Why do you believe you do this? Discuss.

_____

_____

_____

_____

_____

_____

_____

_____

_____

_____

_____

_____

Day 33

From the lens of your personal routine, can you see a link between the routine and your main source of income or a link between your personal routine and creating money? Can your personal routine support a secondary income if you have, or would like, one? Reflect on whether your personal routine is something that would be sustainable if you took on multiple sources of income. Does it help or hinder each source? Can it be tweaked to allow you to take on multiple sources of income as you grow?

_____

_____

_____

_____

_____

_____

_____

_____

_____

_____

Activity

Observe your personal routine today, is it something that's become second nature, or do you still push yourself to complete it? Reflect on what it might take to create a personal routine for every new source of income you wish to gain. Are you willing to take that on to make more money?

_____

_____

_____

_____

_____

_____

_____

_____

_____

_____

_____

_____

_____

Day 34

What are you afraid will happen if you lose your primary income? What fears do you have about your own routines and how they affect your income? Routines like compulsive shopping, always having the most expensive tech, the newest shoes, addictions, or simple stupidity can all squander a great income. What if having these routines has actually stopped you from creating new sources of income? If you could create new sources of income, would you give up these routines? Could you?

_____

_____

_____

_____

_____

_____

_____

_____

_____

_____

Activity

What do you regularly spend on that is not considered an expense? List out the things you buy regularly that isn't an expense in your eyes. If these things were not purchased, could the income you save, be used differently?

_____

_____

_____

_____

_____

_____

_____

_____

_____

_____

_____

_____

_____

_____

Day 35

There are not many ways to make a living without being in contact with someone. Whether it be your family or your friends, your clients or your co-workers, being a part of a team is an important aspect of making a living. How do you view your community through the lens of your income? Does your community routine include a member or members from an aspect of your life where you create an income? Plainly, does your community routine create an income? Could the members you've been building trust with support or guide you in a new source of income? Do the people in your life make an income in the same way you do, or in other ways? Could you learn a new way to make an income from them or with them?

_____

_____

_____

_____

_____

_____

_____

_____

_____

_____

_____

Activity

List the people you interact with today or over the next week. How do they make an income? Do you think you know, or do you know exactly how they make an income? Reflect on the difference between what you think you know and what it would take to get the facts.

_____

_____

_____

_____

_____

_____

_____

_____

_____

Day 36

Could you have a conversation with someone in your community about how they create an income? What concerns come up around having this conversation? What would it mean if someone asked you how you created money? Discover the fears you have around talking about money with others. What would you be comfortable disclosing and what would you never discuss. Vice versa, what would you be willing to ask, and what kind of relationship would you need to have in order to be comfortable asking?

_____

_____

_____

_____

_____

_____

_____

_____

_____

_____

_____

Activity

Take a leap of faith and start a conversation about money with someone today. Share what you've been discovering through you entries in this journal. Take the conversation one step beyond what you feel comfortable asking, however that might look for you.

_____

_____

_____

_____

_____

_____

_____

_____

_____

_____

_____

_____

_____

_____

Day 37

Your financial routine should be directly impacting your income. Whatever you chose to perform you should have a better understanding of your income and/or be more aware of it's actual flow, coming in from your source(s) of income and flowing out to your expenses. Can your current financial routine support a secondary income or multiple sources, can it sustain creating new sources of income? In what ways could it be expanded to maintain your income or enhance sources of income you wish to create?

_____

_____

_____

_____

_____

_____

_____

_____

_____

_____

Activity

Based on the impacts your financial routine has had on your money, had it changed your everyday life. Does your newfound awareness foster relief or worry? Would this change with multiple sources and if so, how?

_____

_____

_____

_____

_____

_____

_____

_____

_____

_____

_____

_____

_____

Day 38

What is your biggest concern about your income? Can you see yourself being someone with multiple sources of income? Can you manage everything that may be needed in order to have multiple sources? What feelings and emotions show up when you read "manage everything," and "multiple sources." Do you believe in some way that people who have more money or more sources of income, do more than you do with the same hours in the day? Reflect on what makes you different from someone with more money or more sources of income? When did you started believing this?

_____

_____

_____

_____

_____

_____

_____

_____

_____

_____

Activity

Who do you admire in your life that has a great income. If this is someone you know, reach out to them to discuss it. If it's a celebrity or world leader, do some research about their early life. In either case compare their early life to yours. Reflect on similarities and differences.

_____

_____

_____

_____

_____

_____

_____

_____

_____

_____

_____

_____

_____

_____

Day 39- Saving

What does savings mean to you? Does it mean a rainy day fund, putting aside some income, or is it more structured like a retirement plan? What is your first memory of saving? Maybe it was a piggy bank, or a special box for birthday money. Why were you saving at that age? What do you remember being told about saving from the adults around you? Why do you save today? Has your reason for saving changed? Explore your beliefs on saving today.

_____

_____

_____

_____

_____

_____

_____

_____

_____

_____

_____

Activity

If you are currently saving, what are you saving for and how long have you been saving? When will this savings be used and will the purpose continue to allow you to save or not?

_____

_____

_____

_____

_____

_____

_____

_____

_____

_____

_____

_____

_____

Day 40

Similar to expenses, savings can be something short term or long term, and even last forever. Some people save forever just because that's what they know to do. Others save for short term items and then purchase those items and go back to saving for the next thing. The same can be said for long term savings, simply with a different frequency. What does saving in the future look like to you? What would you be saving for in the future? On the flip side, if you choose to, why wouldn't you save for the future, what stops you from thinking it's necessary.

_____

_____

_____

_____

_____

_____

_____

_____

_____

Activity

Whether you save for the future or not, notice how it affects your day today and whether or not you look forward to the future. Do you think saving now for the future makes sense or savings at some point in the future is your goal? There is no right answer, only what you discover about yourself.

_____

_____

_____

_____

_____

_____

_____

_____

_____

_____

_____

_____

_____

Day 41

Whether you save now or in the future what are the options you're aware of for saving. It could be with the bank, or in an investment, or even under your mattress. If you do save or could be saving where would you prefer to save it? What are the pros and cons of saving your money in these places? What are the levels of trust you attribute to these places and why? Where did this trust come from? Usually trust begins at an early age from the suggestions and recommendations of adults. Trust, though hard to foster, can easily be lost and in some cases losing ones savings can turn you away from an savings option forever. Reflect on this.

_____

_____

_____

_____

_____

_____

_____

_____

_____

_____

Activity

Observe the trust you have for different ways to save your money. Where do you have your money right now? Would you move your money to other places for the right reasons? Does where you move your money depend on trust, being right, or the fear of losing it?

_____

_____

_____

_____

_____

_____

_____

_____

_____

_____

_____

_____

_____

Day 42

We've discussed what you think of savings, whether it be now or in the future. We've looked at different places to save and how and why you trust these places. What will you do with your savings? Outside of saving for bigger purchases, what are other ways a large sum of savings can be used for? What if your savings could continue to grow without having to save forever? Creating a business or investing can allow ones savings to grow rather than simply remain untouched for a rainy day or slowly reduced with expenses and purchases. Reflect on what it would feel like to always know your savings was growing even if you stopped saving.

Activity

As you go through today, what would be different during your day to day life if your savings was constantly growing each day. Similar to working and earning an income, instead your savings was now growing at the same rate or more. Describe how life might be different.

Day 43

Has your savings been impacted by your personal routine? Has your personal routine allowed you to save in another way? Looking at your personal routine how can you link it to your savings. What new personal routines could you create to save more, or start saving? What routines have you used in the past that simply did not work? Discuss.

_____

_____

_____

_____

_____

_____

_____

_____

_____

_____

_____

Activity

Check in with your personal routine. Have you continued to perform it as you declared. If so, what have you learned? If not, that's perfectly alright, simply reflect on what hasn't allowed you to continue. Whatever reason this may be, does it stop you in other areas of your life? Explain.

_____

_____

_____

_____

_____

_____

_____

_____

_____

_____

_____

_____

_____

Day 44

What personal fears do you have about savings? Are you the type of person that people know will save or will not? Who in your life is someone labeled as a saver, why? What's the worse thing that could happen to your savings, why would it happen, and how can you ensure it doesn't. How is this fear stopping you from actually saving?

_____

_____

_____

_____

_____

_____

_____

_____

_____

_____

_____

Activity

Throughout today observe others and the way they may save, such as bringing lunches rather than eating out, or bringing a coffee mug rather than buying coffee. What are your thoughts and beliefs about this person? Would you consider them a saver? If you consider yourself to be this person, would you label yourself as a saver? Why or why not?

_____

_____

_____

_____

_____

_____

_____

_____

_____

_____

_____

_____

Day 45

Have you ever considered saving with others? For example pooling your funds to grow a larger pot of money together. Many businesses start this way in order to create a team and ensure that everyone has some vested interest. How do the people in your life save? Could you save with them or learn from them? How has your community routine impacted your savings or allowed you to start to save?

_____

_____

_____

_____

_____

_____

_____

_____

_____

_____

_____

Activity

Learn about where other people have chosen to save and why they've chosen to save there (bank, investments, etc). Regardless of their choice, notice the relationships they describe with their advisers, their mentors and/or other friends they trust. Take note of any repetition throughout the people you speak with.

_____

_____

_____

_____

_____

_____

_____

_____

_____

_____

_____

_____

_____

Day 46

What's fears might you have about saving money with other people, even family members. If you currently save money with others, discuss what you've learned since doing so. Whether you currently do so or not, saving money with new people can be uncomfortable. What would it take for you to save your money with someone else? What do you think would be needed for someone to save money with you, invest with you, start a business with you?

_____

_____

_____

_____

_____

_____

_____

_____

_____

_____

Activity

Make a list of people you'd be willing to save your money with, invest with, start a team or company with. Make another list of the people that would save with you, invest with you, start a team or company with you. Find which names show up on both list. Reflect on the matching names and what that means to you. Reach out to these people and share your thoughts, learning and ideas.

_____

_____

_____

_____

_____

_____

_____

_____

_____

_____

_____

_____

_____

Day 47

What has been the impact on your savings since taking on your financial routine? Has your savings grown or not, have you been able to see changes throughout performing this routine regularly? If you have not been performing this routine, discuss what's been stopping you. If you are performing this routine, what do you foresee in the future.

_____

_____

_____

_____

_____

_____

_____

_____

_____

_____

_____

Activity

Take a moment to measure the impact on your savings since beginning your financial routine. What is the amount? What do you intend to do about the changes? What have you learned so far? Share this impact with someone in your community.

_____

_____

_____

_____

_____

_____

_____

_____

_____

_____

_____

_____

_____

Day 48

What amount of your savings would be OK to risk, or lose, possibly in an investment or company? What amount would be too much to risk? In contrast what amount of gain would be worth the risk of losing? If you lost all your savings what would that mean about you? What would it mean about you to your community? Who would you be? What if your risk paid off, who would you be then? Discover how the fear of risk might be stopping you not just in your finances but in other areas of your life. Think back to an opportunity that may have been offered to you, but you did not take because the risk was too great. Describe the incident and how you experienced it.

_____

_____

_____

_____

_____

_____

_____

_____

_____

_____

_____

Activity

As you go through your day, take a moment to think about what would change if you'd lost all your savings. If you're savings either now or whatever you intend to save in the future, were lost. How would it affect a day like today, or your everyday routines. Explain below.

_____

_____

_____

_____

_____

_____

_____

_____

_____

_____

_____

Day 49 - Budget

Today you're going to begin to take everything you've discovered so far and draft out a budget. Usually when you hear budget, you see numbers, spreadsheets and dollar signs. Take control on your finances by looking at them monthly. We will complete creating this over the next little while, so don't expect to have it all done in one sitting. What you think a budget is? Reflect on whether your view of a budget has changed over time. Would have included medium expenses? Would you have thought about unknown expenses?

_____

_____

_____

_____

_____

_____

_____

_____

_____

Activity

What do you think a budget should include? How simply or complex should it be? What would you include in a budget?

_____

_____

_____

_____

_____

_____

_____

_____

_____

_____

_____

_____

_____

_____

Day 50

Today we're looking at the expenses area of the budget. How did you see expenses before using this journal? What did you think about expenses before reading this journal? Did you learn anything new about expenses?

_____

_____

_____

_____

_____

_____

_____

_____

_____

_____

_____

_____

Activity

Take some time to fill in the Expenses area of your budget using the last page as a guide. Ensure that if you are looking at daily or weekly expenses, you add them up to ensure they can be included as a monthly total. Reflect below on the expenses you currently incur.

_____

_____

_____

_____

_____

_____

_____

_____

_____

_____

_____

_____

_____

Day 51

Looking at income today what have you learned so far about your source of income? Have you seen opportunities to create a second income or multiple sources of income? If you have, what would it take to create those new sources?

_____

_____

_____

_____

_____

_____

_____

_____

_____

_____

_____

_____

_____

Activity

Fill in the income area of your budget worksheet. Be sure to add your income together to create a monthly number to be used on the budget sheet. Reflect below on your source of income.

_____

_____

_____

_____

_____

_____

_____

_____

_____

_____

_____

_____

_____

_____

Day 52

What savings do you currently have? Where do you keep your
savings and is it in a structure you can get to easily? Brainstorm
some areas you'd intend on placing your savings.

_____

_____

_____

_____

_____

_____

_____

_____

_____

_____

_____

Activity

Looking at the expenses you've listed and the income you currently have, complete the math to understand your financial reality. Do you have a surplus of money, or are you in a deficit? Add up all your expenses and subtract it from your income, this is your financial reality. Discuss any initial thoughts after doing the math.

_____

_____

_____

_____

_____

_____

_____

_____

_____

_____

_____

_____

_____

Day 53

After creating your current budget and understanding your current financial reality, how do you feel? If you have a surplus of money each month, do you feel like this amount is a true reflection on your bank account? Does you financial reality show that your expenses are greater than your income? In this case, how does it feel to have less than you need? Reflect on your personal scenario.

_____

_____

_____

_____

_____

_____

_____

_____

_____

_____

_____

Activity

Taking your financial reality into account. How much money do you have in surplus each month or how much money do you have in deficit? Take this number and multiply it by 12. How much money would you have in a year in surplus or in deficit? Place this number at the bottom of your budget worksheet. Reflect on this number below.

_____

_____

_____

_____

_____

_____

_____

_____

_____

_____

_____

_____

_____

Community

A community is essential to any leader. With the support of like minded individuals working towards the same goals, anyone can accomplish their goals much faster. Working as a team also allows everyone to bring their unique skills together. One routine we've continued to work through continues to involve the people around you. This important routine will allow you to build a community focused on the same goals you have as well as shared financial security and freedom. As we move through this section, creating a community will be broken down using the same routines we continue to perform. Connecting with people will require knowing who may already be in your community and understanding what your community is focused on. Any similar goals or achievements will allow you to grow your circle, one person at a time. The road toward those achievements usually comes with many forks in the road and having team members will engage communication which will lead to action. We will discuss taking action aligned with your goals and understand that taking no action, is also an action. Next we will spend some time acknowledging ourselves and those around us. A simple thank you can go a very long way. And finally accepting what we've achieved vs simply focusing on the outcomes we've produced will allow the perspective needed to keep moving forward. Let's Begin...

Day 54

Who are in your communities today, your family, your friends, etc? Do you have many different communities or do you tend to simply stick to one? Within those communities, who specifically do you interact with?

_____

_____

_____

_____

_____

_____

_____

_____

_____

_____

_____

_____

_____

Activity

Today recognize the different people you interact with. Your co-workers, your family, your friends are usually the most common, but some not so common could be your barista, your receptionist, or even someone you usually notice on the ride to work. Recognize and reflect on anything you noticed differently.

_____

_____

_____

_____

_____

_____

_____

_____

_____

_____

_____

_____

_____

_____

Day 55

Thinking about the people in your current network, do they support your ideas and goals? If so, discuss how you are encouraged and how this supports your ideas coming true. On the other hand, do the people in your network hinder your progress? If so, reflect on the last great idea you had, and how it felt to share this with your community.

_____

_____

_____

_____

_____

_____

_____

_____

_____

_____

_____

_____

Activity

Thinking about your financial reality, who would you be willing to share the actual numbers with? Who do you feel comfortable with to share whether you can save money each month or if you're actually losing money each month? When it comes to money, who do you trust? Share your financial reality with someone new today. Reflect on what happens.

_____

_____

_____

_____

_____

_____

_____

_____

_____

_____

_____

_____

_____

_____

Day 56

Thinking back to when you created your vision, who were the people you wanted in your community? What community would you be a part of in order to propel yourself forward? Remember that everything that seems normal has gotten you the results you have today. New results require new actions, this means the same is true in your community. What does that mean to you?

_____

_____

_____

_____

_____

_____

_____

_____

_____

_____

_____

_____

Activity

Introduce yourself to someone new today, it could be as simple as your name or as in depth as sharing yourself and who you are vulnerably. Regardless take on adding someone new to your community. Reflect on how you think this will impact your life.

_____

_____

_____

_____

_____

_____

_____

_____

_____

_____

_____

_____

_____

_____

Day 57

How has your personal routine been coming along? If you've continued it, discuss how it's been for you so far. If you haven't continued, explain what's been stopping you and where that same reason stops you elsewhere in your life. Reflect on how your personal routine could support creating new communities.

_____

_____

_____

_____

_____

_____

_____

_____

_____

_____

_____

_____

Activity

Renew your commitment to yourself and your personal routine. Can you enhance your routine in some way, expand it if possible? Share your personal routine with someone and what you've gotten out of performing or what you've learned out of not performing.

_____

_____

_____

_____

_____

_____

_____

_____

_____

_____

_____

_____

_____

_____

Day 58

How has your community routine been coming along? If you've continued it, discuss how it's been for you so far. If you haven't continued, explain what's been stopping you and where that same reason stops you elsewhere in your life. Reflect on whether your community routine has made it easier or harder to meet new people.

_____

_____

_____

_____

_____

_____

_____

_____

_____

_____

_____

_____

Activity

Renew your commitment to yourself and your community routine. Can you enhance your routine in some way, expand it if possible? Share with the person or group you chose as part of your community routine. Explain what you've gotten out of spending time with them or what you've learned out of choosing not to.

_____

_____

_____

_____

_____

_____

_____

_____

_____

_____

_____

_____

_____

_____

Day 59

How has your financial routine been coming along? If you've continued it, discuss how it's been for you so far. If you haven't continued, explain what's been stopping you and where that same reason stops you elsewhere in your life. Explore how your financial routine could support a community. What are your beliefs financially around supporting yourself? What are your beliefs financially around support others?

_____

_____

_____

_____

_____

_____

_____

_____

_____

_____

_____

Activity

Renew your commitment to yourself and your financial routine. Can you enhance your routine in some way, expand it if possible? Share your financial routine with someone new. Explain what you've gotten out of performing your financial routine or what you've learned out of choosing not to.

_____

_____

_____

_____

_____

_____

_____

_____

_____

_____

_____

_____

_____

Day 60

Creating something new can always be challenging at first. Sometimes we look at new opportunities like we've tried them before and therefore we assume the same failures will happen. For the purposes of this journal we will use a new word to create a new understanding for ourselves. This new word is Achievability and we will use it to create something we hope to accomplish. Next we will define what achievability means but before that, describe what you think it means below.

_____

_____

_____

_____

_____

_____

_____

_____

_____

_____

Activity

Today try using a different word for something you usually talk about. Maybe instead of dinner you say supper, or instead of car you say vehicle. Notice where you use the same words, and where you could say something different. When you say something differently, what reactions or responses do you get? Compare these responses to the responses you get when you share new ideas or opportunities with those around you.

_____

_____

_____

_____

_____

_____

_____

_____

_____

_____

_____

_____

_____

Day 61

Within this journal we will define an achievability as the ability or quality you need to achieve the goals you set. For example if you have the goal of buying your dream home it will take new abilities to achieve this. Only you will know what it will take though. Maybe it will take courage, or determination or a combination of these plus more. Describe the abilities you believe you will need.

_____

_____

_____

_____

_____

_____

_____

_____

_____

_____

_____

Activity

Think about the abilities you described above as you go through your day. Where can you easily take on these abilities newly and where might it be challenging? Reflect on what you notice.

_____

_____

_____

_____

_____

_____

_____

_____

_____

_____

_____

_____

_____

_____

_____

Day 62

To create an achievability you declare it. Finish the following sentence: in order to achieve my vision I will be _____. If at any point you don't know what ability or abilities you will need, review your vision. Notice how challenging it may be for you to finish the sentence, what are you telling yourself about simply declaring what you want versus it actually happening. Reflect on this.

in order to achieve my vision I will be _____

_____

_____

_____

_____

_____

_____

_____

_____

_____

_____

_____

Activity

Throughout your day, simply repeat your achievability. Notice and reflect on any changes today through this practice. Notice your immediate reaction after repeating your achievability. What is the immediate feeling or response to yourself?

_____

_____

_____

_____

_____

_____

_____

_____

_____

_____

_____

_____

_____

_____

Day 63

Now that you've declared an achievability, does it align with your personal routine? Use your achievability to enhance or expand your personal routine. As you continue to add different layers to your personal routine, what is showing up in your life?

_____

_____

_____

_____

_____

_____

_____

_____

_____

_____

_____

_____

_____

Activity

As you perform your personal routine today, simply declare your achievability. How does it sound along with performing personal your routine? What have you noticed differently?

_____

_____

_____

_____

_____

_____

_____

_____

_____

_____

_____

_____

_____

_____

Day 64

Does your achievability align with your community routine? Use your achievability to enhance or expand your community routine. How do you think your achievability will enhance your community routine?

_____

_____

_____

_____

_____

_____

_____

_____

_____

_____

_____

Activity

As you perform your community routine today or this week, simply declare your achievability. How does it sound along with performing your community routine? What have you noticed differently? Share your achievability with someone in your community. What did they think?

_____

_____

_____

_____

_____

_____

_____

_____

_____

_____

_____

_____

_____

Day 65

Alongside your personal and community routines, does your achievability statement align with your financial routine? Based on what you created, when declaring your acheivability, do you feel positive and empowered around your financial routine? Reflect on where your financial routine is so far and what do you think your acheivability will bring to it?

_____

_____

_____

_____

_____

_____

_____

_____

_____

_____

_____

_____

Activity

As you perform your financial routine today or this week, simply declare your achievability. How does it sound along with performing your financial routine? What have you noticed differently?

_____

_____

_____

_____

_____

_____

_____

_____

_____

_____

_____

_____

_____

Day 66

Sometimes opportunities show up all at once and other times we sit back, waiting for that big break that never seems to come. What are your ideas and beliefs about opportunities? Where do these beliefs stem from? When did you begin to believe them?

_____

_____

_____

_____

_____

_____

_____

_____

_____

_____

_____

_____

_____

_____

Activity

Today notice where you may already have opportunities in your life. Also notice where you believe there are no opportunities, like at work, or at home. Reflect on the way you see opportunities that show up today and why you see it that way.

_____

_____

_____

_____

_____

_____

_____

_____

_____

_____

_____

_____

_____

Day 67

Now that we can use new words in new ways, we will change the word opportunity to something simpler. Thinking about the significance we give to the word opportunity and what we believe it to mean we will now use the word "forks" in its place. Every now and then we come upon a fork in the road. These forks seem trivial at first but they require a choice. That simple, insignificant, sometimes unthought of choice, ends up being the beginning of a new path in life. Think back to when you chose a school or occupation, which created the community around you today in friends or colleagues. Reflect on some forks in your life and where they've taken you.

_____

_____

_____

_____

_____

_____

_____

_____

_____

Activity

Take a different route to work today or try a new place for lunch. Whatever it may be, take a different fork than you normally would. Reflect on the difference you notice in your day by taking a new fork in the road.

_____

_____

_____

_____

_____

_____

_____

_____

_____

_____

_____

_____

Day 68

Where do forks come from? The forks in our lives are rarely something we see coming, but instead show up looking for choices to be made. When you see a fork in the road, what do you really see? Thinking back to when we used the word opportunity, how do you see both words differently? What does each word mean to you? Why do they hold this meaning?

_____

_____

_____

_____

_____

_____

_____

_____

_____

_____

_____

Activity

Think of an opportunity that presented itself to you recently, what choice did you make? If you thought of that opportunity as a fork in the road, would you have made the same choice? Did you even see the opportunity for what it was, or did you automatically know how it was going to go?

_____

_____

_____

_____

_____

_____

_____

_____

_____

_____

_____

_____

_____

Day 69

Everyday we bring our past experiences with us everywhere. A new job offer might be available, but you already know what that means, more work, possibly moving locations, more pay, more stress. You have the same experiences at home, already knowing what to expect the minute you open the door, the same experiences at the supermarket, the bank, etc. At the beginning of every fork you take a moment to think, does this look familiar, have I done this before, is this safe? The instant something looks, feels, or even smells familiar, you already know exactly how its going to go, and this affects your choice. This colors your choice into doing exactly what you know, inevitably making the same choice you always make. Remember, making the same choices has gotten you the same results. Choosing something new gets you new results. Why do you think you make the same choices?

_____

_____

_____

_____

_____

_____

_____

_____

_____

_____

_____

_____

Activity

In every choice you make today, try making a different one. A choice you wouldn't normally make. What changes did you notice for yourself after making that choice? What were the results of that choice?

_____

_____

_____

_____

_____

_____

_____

_____

_____

_____

Day 70

Making a choice when life brings you to a fork in the road always includes fear. The fear is most often why we analyze, we research, we try to get all the information we need before making that choice. And inevitably we simply make the same choice we would always make. Therefore it isn't the fork or even ourselves that choose, it is our fear. What would it be like if you could make a choice without fear? When you think back to your vision, what fears do you have?

_____

_____

_____

_____

_____

_____

_____

_____

_____

_____

Activity

Today or throughout this week when forks arise, simply say yes.
Don't think, don't analyze, don't even skip a beat. Try just saying
yes. What did you say yes to? What impact does that have on your
life? How did it feel to make a choice without fear setting in?

_____

_____

_____

_____

_____

_____

_____

_____

_____

_____

_____

_____

_____

_____

Day 71

When forks arise in our lives we automatically believe that a choice has to be made. Sometimes the window to make that choice slips away and we can no longer make a choice. Often we believe if we haven't made a choice then there is no impact on us. This would be incorrect. Not making a choice is still a choice and it can make just as strong of an impact. Think back to when you did not make a choice even though you could have. How long did it take to choose you were not making a choice? What impacts did it have on you? How long did not making a choice impact you? If applicable, what impacts did it have on your community or your finances? How long as that impacted your community and/or your finances?

_____

_____

_____

_____

_____

_____

_____

_____

Activity

Today reflect on the choices you usually make or have to make on a regular basis. How many people are impacted by whether you make a choice or not? How do you feel about making these choices? What does it mean about you, whether you make a choice or not?

Day 72

In most cases saying yes will require you to take actions or fulfill on a promise. Would you consider yourself hard worker? When making a choice do you factor in how much work it will take to fulfill on your promise? Where in life does the work not matter, you don't care how much work it takes, you will stop at nothing to fulfill on your promise. In what areas of life does it matter? Compare your life in both contexts.

_____

_____

_____

_____

_____

_____

_____

_____

_____

_____

_____

Activity

Take note of all the things you're doing today. Which areas do you consider work? Your job, your hobbies, your errands? Which areas don't you consider work? Family, friends, etc. Compare them, along with your ability to perform them and why they are important.

_____

_____

_____

_____

_____

_____

_____

_____

_____

_____

_____

_____

_____

Day 73

Are you a person who keeps their word? Can you be trusted to complete a task? What stops you from completing a task on time? Do people believe they can trust you?

_____

_____

_____

_____

_____

_____

_____

_____

_____

_____

_____

_____

_____

Activity

Make a promise today. Give your word to someone. By the end of the day fulfill on that promise. Reflect on how your day went from making to fulfilling on that promise.

_____

_____

_____

_____

_____

_____

_____

_____

_____

_____

_____

_____

_____

_____

Day 74

Fulfilling on a promise you made can be very rewarding. Sometimes we believe we've taken all the actions needed to complete on a promise, but then it is reviewed, criticized and needs to be reworked, redone, or started over. When have you made a promise and knew exactly what it was going to take to fulfill on that promise? When have you completed on that promise only to have be criticized for not meeting all expectations?

_____

_____

_____

_____

_____

_____

_____

_____

_____

_____

_____

Activity

Think about all the different promises you've made that you are currently working on. Are there any where you believe you know how to meet all expectations? Are there any where you could review the promise made to ensure you're clear. Discuss what you discovered by reviewing the promise you made.

_____

_____

_____

_____

_____

_____

_____

_____

_____

_____

_____

_____

_____

Day 75

Sometimes we only make connections backwards. For example, choosing a specific profession got you to the city you live in, and the living situation you're in, etc. Sometimes we look back and think what would have happened had a different choice been made. In reality we would never know how exactly making a different choice would have changed our lives. The only thing we know for sure is that all our choices brought us to this point. Reflect on your life today, and map out the actions you took. What choices did you make which had you take those actions? What fork in the road had you make those choices? Thinking to the fork in the road that had you go on this path, what do you think your achievability needed to be in order to take that first step forward? Reflect on entire process below.

_____

_____

_____

_____

_____

_____

_____

_____

_____

_____

_____

Activity

Look back on today or yesterday and map out the route you took to work, or the choices you made at work or at home. Use your day as a smaller example of connecting the dots backwards. Think about the actions you took throughout your day, the choices you made that had you take those actions, the forks in your day where you had to choose, and what achievability you started the day with or may have needed? Seen another way:

Acheivability>Forks>Choices>Actions>Your Life

_____

_____

_____

_____

_____

_____

_____

_____

_____

Day 76

Every day we go through similar or the same motions. Days turns to months that turn into years. Sometimes we feel like we're winning and other times, not so much. At any point in time how often do we stop to acknowledge ourselves for the things they've done. How often do you acknowledge yourself? Do you see any connections?

_____

_____

_____

_____

_____

_____

_____

_____

_____

_____

_____

_____

Activity

Take a moment today to acknowledge the people in your life. Whether it be grabbing your morning coffee, in your meetings, at home, or wherever you see the opportunity. Simply say thank you, take a moment to acknowledge, or spend some time in appreciation. Explain how this action impacted you and your day.

_____

_____

_____

_____

_____

_____

_____

_____

_____

_____

_____

_____

_____

Day 77

Taking a moment to acknowledge yourself is the first step toward accepting your achievements and outcomes. What do you believe achievements to be? What do you believe outcomes to be? How are they different?

_____

_____

_____

_____

_____

_____

_____

_____

_____

_____

_____

_____

Activity

Chat with someone today about what they think achievements and outcomes to be. Are their definitions similar or different from yours? What do you agree on and what do you disagree on?

_____

_____

_____

_____

_____

_____

_____

_____

_____

_____

_____

_____

_____

_____

_____

Day 78

Remember when we created using the word achievability, the ability to achieve. By using a new word we can look at achievements in a new way or any way we want. Think about your greatest achievement. What did it take to make that happen? Did people see you differently, did you see yourself differently? Discuss below.

_____

_____

_____

_____

_____

_____

_____

_____

_____

_____

_____

_____

Activity

Sometimes achievements can be grand goals we have that take years to complete. Achievements can also be simple things that happen each day. Reflect on everything that happened today and write your greatest achievement from today only.

_____

_____

_____

_____

_____

_____

_____

_____

_____

_____

_____

_____

_____

_____

Day 79

Outcomes occur when actions are taken but they are distinct from achievements. Outcomes are the real, physical things that come from our actions. For example, writing a book would result in the outcome of having a physical book, printed with words on the page, or maybe a digital e-version. This is distinct from the achievement of writing a book as the author now knows them self in a new way. Review the example you discussed before, your greatest achievement for the day. This time reflect on what you achieved and what were your outcomes.

_____

_____

_____

_____

_____

_____

_____

_____

_____

Activity

Completing the same activity as before look at all the activities that happened today. Discuss your achievements and outcomes and how they are different. Can you have an Achievement without an outcome or an outcome without and achievement?

_____

_____

_____

_____

_____

_____

_____

_____

_____

_____

_____

_____

_____

_____

Day 80

What have you achieved since taking on this journal? Think through your routines, personal, community and financial. What have been your achievements?

_____

_____

_____

_____

_____

_____

_____

_____

_____

_____

Activity

Take some time today to share your achievements with someone. Ask whether they see these as achievements too. Ask what they have achieved in the same time period.

_____

_____

_____

_____

_____

_____

_____

_____

_____

_____

_____

_____

_____

Day 81

What have been your outcomes since taking on this journal? Think through your routines, personal, community and financial. What have been your outcomes?

_____

_____

_____

_____

_____

_____

_____

_____

_____

_____

_____

_____

_____

Activity

Take some time today to share your outcomes with someone. Ask whether they see these as outcomes too. Ask what have been their outcomes in the same time period.

_____

_____

_____

_____

_____

_____

_____

_____

_____

_____

_____

_____

_____

_____

Reflect

As the journal is concluded it is important to take a step back and realize everything it took to complete something you intended for such a long period of time. Many people around you may not know the effort and time it took you to get to this page. They may only see the outcomes whereas you see the achievements. They may not see anything at all, but you know that structures now exist, foundations have been laid and it's only a matter of time before the vision you created is the reality you're living. Over the next little while you will be reflecting. Share what you've learned, share what it took and share the things that your community may not know. Your leadership is certain in the community you created, your words are powerful as you know yourself not only to be someone who can now guide and support others, but also someone who completed on their word. You are near the finish line, finish strong and reflect on the person who you were at the start of this journal. That person may not even be someone you recognize anymore and that's alright, as your character grows, so has your finances. Let's Begin...

Day 82

Read through your vision. Reflect on what you remember when you began writing it. What has changed since then? How much of it has become a reality? How much of it is there to still become a reality? What would you change or enhance? Reflect on your journey with this journal, through your vision.

_____

_____

_____

_____

_____

_____

_____

_____

_____

_____

_____

_____

_____

Activity

Does life seem different than it did when you first began this journal? If it has, explain why you feel it has. If it hasn't, explain why you feel it hasn't. Whether it's changed or not, notice whether this is a completely new experience for you because you took completely new actions. If it hasn't changed, notice where your actions may have been more of the same.

_____

_____

_____

_____

_____

_____

_____

_____

_____

_____

_____

_____

_____

_____

Day 83

Take a moment to read through your entries on starting habits. How did you feel about starting a new habit then? How do you feel about starting a new one now? If you kept up with your habits, what were your achievements, what were your outcomes? What does this new confidence bring you? Reflect on your journey with habits.

_____

_____

_____

_____

_____

_____

_____

_____

_____

_____

_____

_____

Activity

Look for areas today to start a new habit in your life. It can be in any area, just remember to keep it consistent. Have this new habit further expand yourself toward your vision. Explain what this new habit will be and how it will expand your vision.

_____

_____

_____

_____

_____

_____

_____

_____

_____

_____

_____

_____

_____

_____

Day 84

Flip through your entries on Expenses. Looking back, how do you feel about expenses today? What's the most significant thing that has changed in your life since completing that section? What surprised you about Expenses? How do you see expenses now? Reflect on your journey with expenses.

_____

_____

_____

_____

_____

_____

_____

_____

_____

_____

_____

_____

Activity

Throughout your day, what has changed in your daily view on expenses? Which expenses do you focus on most? What do you see for yourself in the future around Expenses? How will expenses play a role in your vision?

_____

_____

_____

_____

_____

_____

_____

_____

_____

_____

_____

_____

_____

_____

_____

Day 85

Look back on your entries about income. What does your income look like today? What did your income look like when you began that section? Do you have multiple sources of income? Do you intend to add more sources in the future? Reflect on your journey with income.

_____

_____

_____

_____

_____

_____

_____

_____

_____

_____

_____

_____

_____

Activity

Do you see areas in your life where a new source of income could be generated from? Throughout your day, where could you see yourself focusing on creating new sources of income with a vision, new habits, and a community?

_____

_____

_____

_____

_____

_____

_____

_____

_____

_____

_____

_____

_____

_____

Day 86

Reread your entries on savings. What was the state of your savings before beginning this journal? Where were your savings when you began that section? Where are your savings now? While working through this journal what have you learned about savings and how do you intend to save in the future?

_____

_____

_____

_____

_____

_____

_____

_____

_____

_____

_____

_____

Activity

What do you plan on saving up for? Today be generous with someone, buy them a coffee or pay for their lunch. Does it feel different today than it did the last time you paid for someone else? Explain.

_____

_____

_____

_____

_____

_____

_____

_____

_____

_____

_____

_____

_____

Day 87

Take a moment to look at your budget. Since creating it, how closely has it been followed? What adjustments have you had to make? Did your budget help or hinder your financial situation? Do you feel it's important to follow a budget, or not?

_____

_____

_____

_____

_____

_____

_____

_____

_____

_____

_____

_____

Activity

Discuss your budget with someone today. Discover if they have a budget. Is it something they've written down or simply something in their head? Listen for what budgeting means to them, and share what budgeting has done for you.

_____

_____

_____

_____

_____

_____

_____

_____

_____

_____

_____

_____

_____

Day 88

How has your community changed since beginning this journal? Look back on your entries from the beginning of the community routine, how has your community changed? Who is in your life that you included in your vision? Who have you yet to meet? What communities do you interact with now?

_____

_____

_____

_____

_____

_____

_____

_____

_____

_____

_____

_____

Activity

Today think about your usual activities throughout the day and the regular people you always see. What would it take to meet new people, maybe even meet the people you included in your vision? How would your activities today change? What could you do differently?

_____

_____

_____

_____

_____

_____

_____

_____

_____

_____

_____

_____

_____

Day 89

What have you been able to achieve since beginning this journal. Look back at the entries based on the achievability you created. Have you created any new achievabilities since, or have you stuck with the same one? How has the achievability statement helped you throughout this journal?

_____

_____

_____

_____

_____

_____

_____

_____

_____

_____

_____

_____

Activity

Create a new achievability statement just for today. Bring it to every conversation and activity. As you presence the statement, what changes throughout your day?

Today   in   order   to   achieve   my   vision   I   will   be
_____

_____

_____

_____

_____

_____

_____

_____

_____

_____

_____

Day 90

Simply choosing to take on this journal was a fork. What other forks have shown up since beginning to use this journal? Which forks took some time to think about and which ones did you jump right into? Reflect on your experiences based on how you made your choice. Which process worked best for you and why?

_____

_____

_____

_____

_____

_____

_____

_____

_____

_____

_____

_____

_____

Activity

Take some time today to look at the different forks that got you to this day, this point in time. What would you attribute to your success and what would you attribute to your challenges?

_____

_____

_____

_____

_____

_____

_____

_____

_____

_____

_____

_____

_____

_____

Day 91

Whether you took some time to think through your forks or you jumped right in, only you will know the time it took completing the actions to fulfill on that choice. As you review your entries on taking action earlier, do you feel that taking more action or less action would yield the same outcome?

_____

_____

_____

_____

_____

_____

_____

_____

_____

_____

_____

_____

Activity

Have your daily actions changed in any significant way? Since taking on this journal has your day changed? Have your regular actions changed? Reflect back on what has changed around your actions since Day 1.

_____

_____

_____

_____

_____

_____

_____

_____

_____

_____

_____

_____

_____

_____

Day 92

Take some time to acknowledge how far you've come so far. Getting here is no small feat and fulfilling on your promise to complete this journal should not be taken lightly. How do you view acknowledgment today and how has that changed since starting this journal? Where does acknowledgment exist now in your life?

_____

_____

_____

_____

_____

_____

_____

_____

_____

_____

_____

_____

_____

Activity

Take an extra moment today to acknowledge the people around you. Unless you've continued this practice, you may not have done this since the last activity promoting acknowledgement. What do you see that might make acknowledgement challenging? How do you see yourself applying acknowledgment throughout your life?

_____

_____

_____

_____

_____

_____

_____

_____

_____

_____

_____

_____

_____

Day 93

As we near the end of this journal how have you been able to distinguish accomplishments from outcomes? Does the difference exist for you? Before we dig into your achievements and outcomes it is important the we are grounded in the difference. Explain the difference to you, below.

_____

_____

_____

_____

_____

_____

_____

_____

_____

_____

_____

_____

Activity

Today look for the achievements in your day and contrast them to your outcomes. Do you feel any differently based on whether you've had an outcome or whether you've achieved?

_____

_____

_____

_____

_____

_____

_____

_____

_____

_____

_____

_____

_____

_____

Day 94

Since beginning this journal you've had many outcomes in your life. What have been the most significant outcomes? What outcomes surprised you? What outcomes did you intend?

_____

_____

_____

_____

_____

_____

_____

_____

_____

_____

_____

_____

_____

_____

Activity

Reflect today on the outcomes you've had. What outcomes do you see after completing this journal? What would you need to ensure those outcomes happen? How could you continue the principles of this journal after using it?

_____

_____

_____

_____

_____

_____

_____

_____

_____

_____

_____

_____

_____

_____

Day 95

Completing this journal has been an incredible achievement. What have been the most significant achievements since beginning? What achievements surprised you? What did you hope to achieve when you opened the cover?

_____

_____

_____

_____

_____

_____

_____

_____

_____

_____

_____

_____

_____

_____

Activity

Reflect on all your achievements. What do you hope to achieve after completing this journal? What would you need to ensure your achievements remain important to you?

_____

_____

_____

_____

_____

_____

_____

_____

_____

_____

_____

_____

_____

Day 96

What have you learned from performing your personal routine? How has it affected your community? How has it affected your finances? How have you been able to enhance or improve your personal routine throughout this journal?

_____

_____

_____

_____

_____

_____

_____

_____

_____

_____

_____

_____

Activity

Does your personal routine align with your vision? What new personal routines could you take on to come closer to your vision?

_____

_____

_____

_____

_____

_____

_____

_____

_____

_____

_____

_____

_____

_____

Day 97

What have you learned from performing your community routine? How has it affected you personally? How has it affected your finances? How have you been able to enhance or improve your community routine throughout this journal?

_____

_____

_____

_____

_____

_____

_____

_____

_____

_____

_____

_____

Activity

Does your community routine align with your vision? What new community routines could you take on to come closer to your vision?

_____

_____

_____

_____

_____

_____

_____

_____

_____

_____

_____

_____

_____

_____

Day 98

What have you learned from performing your financial routine? How has it affected your community? How has it affected you personally? How have you been able to enhance or improve your financial routine throughout this journal?

_____

_____

_____

_____

_____

_____

_____

_____

_____

_____

_____

_____

Activity

Does your financial routine align with your vision? What new financial routines could you take on to come closer to your vision?

_____

_____

_____

_____

_____

_____

_____

_____

_____

_____

_____

_____

_____

_____

_____

Day 99

How often do you reflect on your life? What parts of your life might you reflect on more than others? Why? Reflecting on your entries throughout this journal, taking into account everything, what has been the most surprising? What did you already know was going to happen?

_____

_____

_____

_____

_____

_____

_____

_____

_____

_____

_____

_____

_____

Activity

Take a moment today to answer the following questions in detail:

1. I am . . .
2. I created . . .
3. I have achieved . . .

_____

_____

_____

_____

_____

_____

_____

_____

_____

_____

_____

_____

_____

Day 100

Take the activity you did yesterday and compare it to your entry from Day 1. What similarities do you see on who you wrote you were on Day 1 and who you are today? What differences are there? What similarities do you see from what you said you created and what you have created? What differences are there? What similarities do you see from what you said you achieved and what you have achieved today?

_____

_____

_____

_____

_____

_____

_____

_____

_____

_____

_____

_____

Activity

Review your vision today. How far have you come since beginning this journal? Take a moment to acknowledge your hard work and dedication to your life and your vision. Your personal, community and financial routines have inevitably impacted the reality of your vision. Whatever is left to achieve will simply take time. How do you intend to stick with it?

_____

_____

_____

_____

_____

_____

_____

_____

_____

_____

_____

_____

About the Author

Yohan Mohammed resides in the suburbs of Toronto, Ontario, Canada. He is a certified teacher of English Literature, Serial Entrepreneur and Philanthropist. An avid traveler, Yohan seeks out the road less traveled experiencing culture, religion, food and most importantly people to understand what drives them toward their own aspirations. Coming from humble beginnings, he has used the same process discussed in this book, on numerous occasions to create new relationships to money, life and love. He writes to share his own experiences and illustrate, that what we truly want doesn't require years of wanting it, but instead days of taking action on it.

My Budget

Expenses

_____

_____

_____

_____

_____

_____

_____

Income

_____

_____

_____

_____

_____

_____

_____

Financial Reality

_____

_____

12 Month Total

_____

_____

CPSIA information can be obtained
at www.ICGtesting.com
Printed in the USA
LVHW112122310519
619789LV00001B/23/P